01 Classical Themes for Busk

Piano/Organ Edition with

The compositions in this book have been freely adapted and simplified for playing in busking style.

Exclusive Distributors:
Music Sales Limited
8/9 Frith Street, London W1V 5TZ, England.
Music Sales Corporation
24 East 22nd Street, New York, N.Y. 10010, USA.
Music Sales Pty. Limited
27 Clarendon Street, Artarmon, Sydney, NSW 2064, Australia.

ISBN 0.7119.1102.9
Order No. AM 65319

Art direction by Mike Bell.
Cover illustration by Graham Thompson.
Compiled & arranged by Peter Lavender.
Music processed by Hillmob Music Services & MSS Studios.

Printed in England by
The Anchor Press Limited, Tiptree, Essex.

Wise Publications
London/New York/Sydney/Cologne

Arditi
1. **Il Bacio**

Bach
2. **Minuet In G Major**
3. **Air On The G String**

Gounod/Bach
4. **Ave Maria (based on Bach's Prelude No. 1 in C Major)**

Beethoven
5. **Für Elise**
6. **Minuet In G**
7. **Adagio (from 'Sonata Pathétique')**
8. **Ode To Joy (theme from Symphony No. 9)**

Bizet
9. **Toreador's Song (from 'Carmen')**

Borodin
10. **Nocturne (from 'String Quartet'**
11. **Polovtsian Dance (from 'Prince Igor')**

Brahms
12. **Hungarian Dance No. 5**
13. **Hungarian Dance No. 6**
14. **Waltz**
15. **Lullaby**

Chopin
16. **Prelude**
17. **Minute Waltz**
18. **Etude**
19. **Fantaisie Impromptu**
20. **Military Polonaise**
21. **Polonaise Opus 53**

Clarke
22. **Trumpet Voluntary**

Debussy
23. **Clair De Lune**
24. **Reverie**

Delibes
25. **Pas Des Fleurs**
26. **Pizzicati (from 'Sylvia')**
27. **Valse Lente (from 'Coppélia')**

Delius
29. **La Calinda**

Di Capua
30. **O Sole Mio**

Drigo
28. **Serenade (from 'Millions D'Arlequin')**

Dvořák
31. **Largo ('From The New World')**
32. **Songs My Mother Taught Me**
33. **Humoresque**

Elgar
34. **Land Of Hope And Glory (Pomp & Circumstance March No. 1)**
35. **Chanson De Matin**

Fibich
36. **Poème**

Fucik
37. **Entry Of The Gladiators**

Gounod
39. **Waltz (from 'Faust')**

Grieg
40. **Anitra's Dance**

Handel
41. **Largo**

Haydn
38. **The Surprise Symphony**

Herbert
42. **Gypsy Love Song**

Holst
44. **I Vow To Thee My Country (theme from 'Jupiter')**

Ivanovici
43. **Waves Of The Danube**

Khachaturian
45. **Spartacus (theme from)**

Leoncavallo
46. **Mattinata**

Liszt
47. **Liebestraum**

MacDowell
48. **To A Wild Rose**

Martini
49. **Plaisir D'Amour**

Il Bacio

Composed by Luigi Arditi

2

Minuet In G Major

Composed by Johann Sebastian Bach

3

Air On The G String

Composed by Johann Sebastian Bach

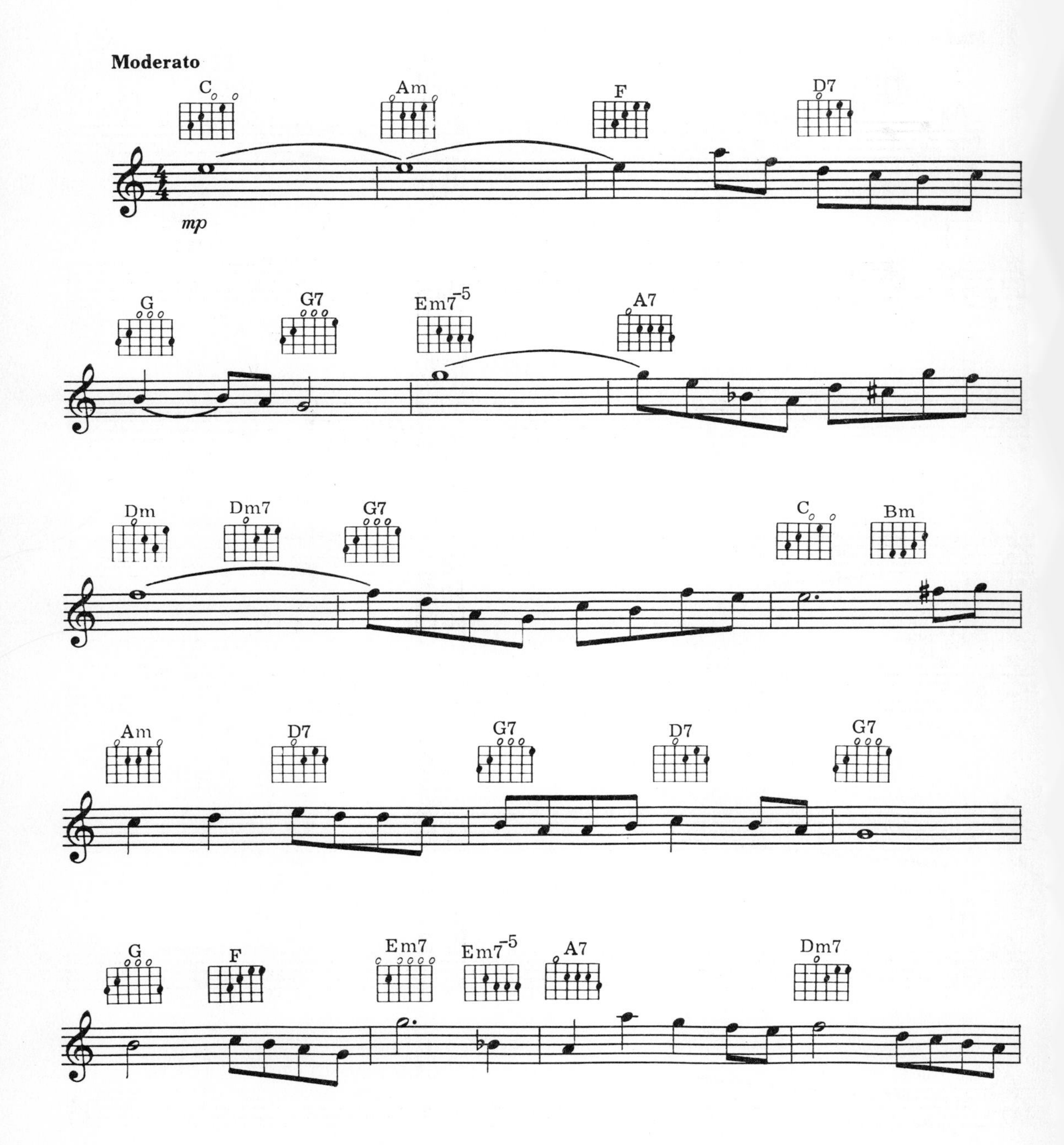

E7 Am E7
Am D7
G D7 G G7 C F D7 G
E7 A7 Dm Dm7 G7
C C7 F C F
Dm Dm7 G7 C

Ave Maria

(based on Bach's Prelude No. 1 in C Major)

Composed by Charles Gounod

5

Für Elise

Composed by Ludwig van Beethoven

Minuet In G

Composed by Ludwig van Beethoven

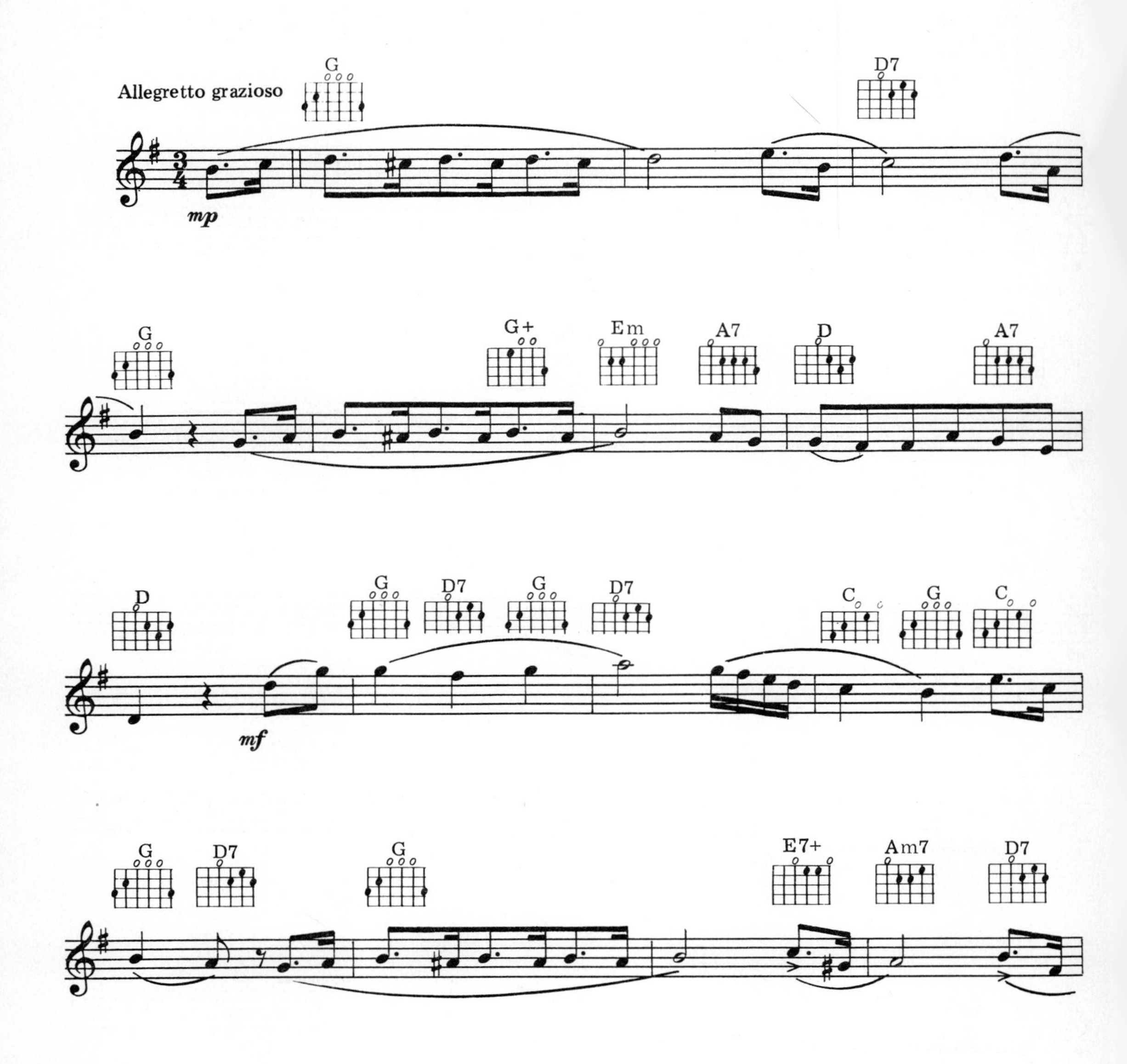

G
D7
G
D7
G
Fine
mp
D7
G
Em7
A7
D
Em
A
D
D7
mf
G
C
D
G
D.C. al Fine
mf

Adagio
(from Sonata Pathétique)
Composed by Ludwig van Beethoven

Ode To Joy
(theme from Symphony No. 9)
Composed by Ludwig van Beethoven

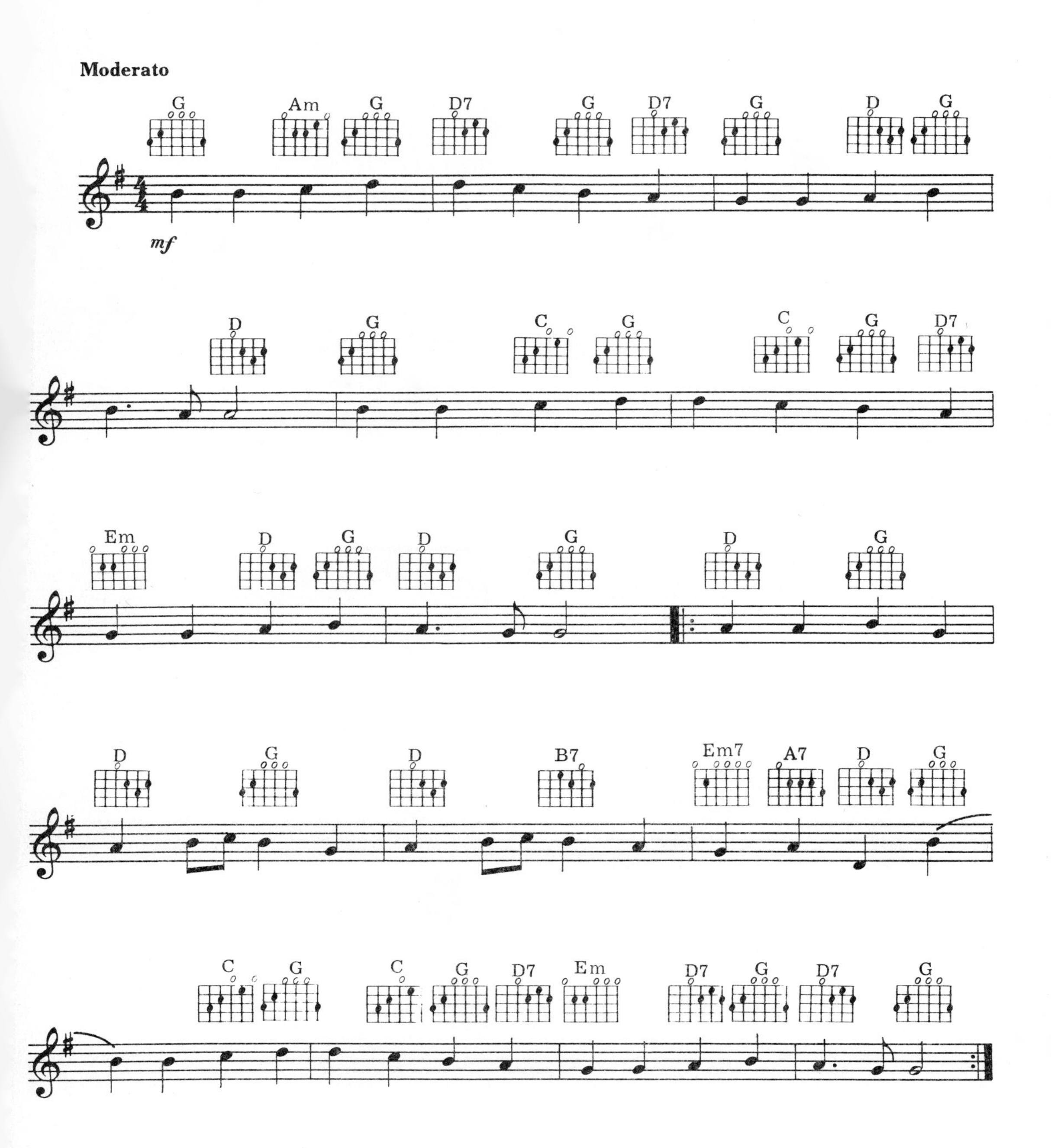

Toreador's Song
(from 'Carmen')

Composed by Georges Bizet

Nocturne
(from String Quartet)
Composed by Alexander Borodin

11

Polovtsian Dance
(from 'Prince Igor')
Composed by Alexander Borodin

F
Gm7
C7
F
Dm7
Gm7
Am7
D7
Gm7
C7
F
Dm7
Gm7
C7
Gb7
F

Hungarian Dance No. 5

Composed by Johannes Brahms

C
F
C
G7
C
G7
C
F
G7
C
G7
C
F
C
G7
C
G7
C
F
G7
C
G7
C
D. C. al Coda
CODA
Fm
G7
Cm

Hungarian Dance No. 6

Composed by Johannes Brahms

14

Waltz

Composed by Johannes Brahms

15

Lullaby

Composed by Johannes Brahms

16

Prelude

Composed by Frederic Chopin

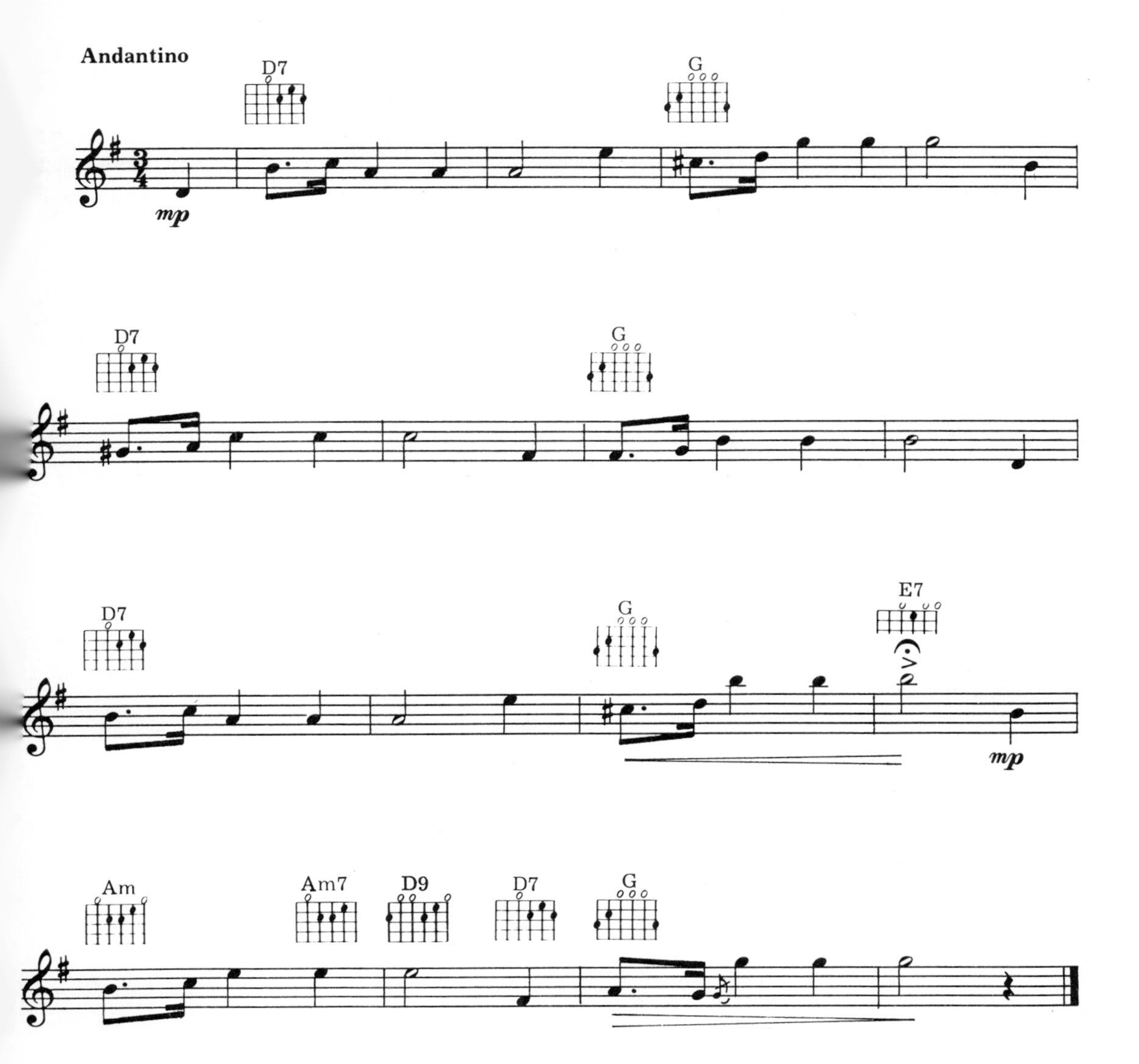

17
Minute Waltz

Composed by Frederic Chopin

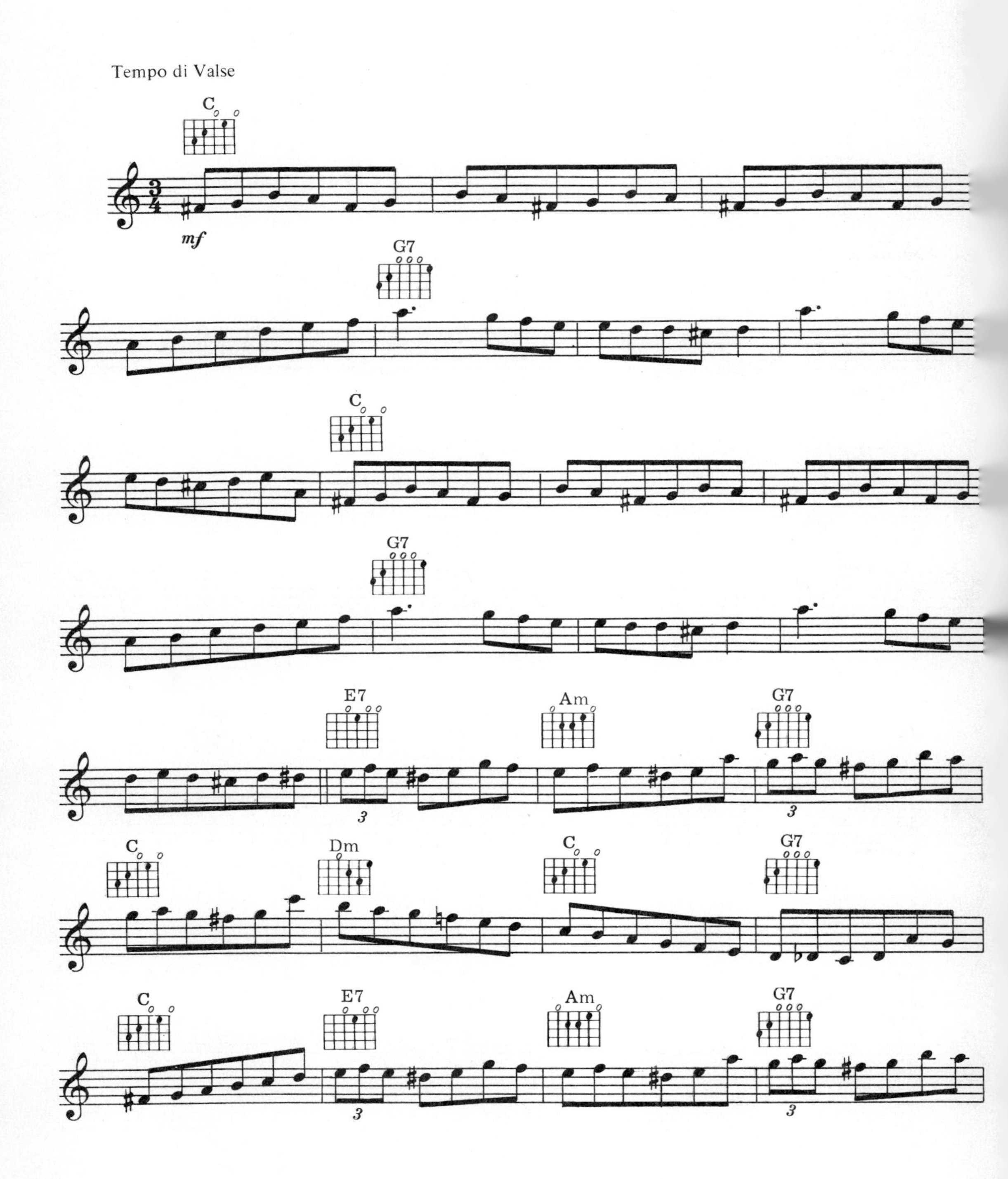

C
Dm7
C
G7
C
Fine
G7
G7+
C
G7
C
F♯o
G7
G7+
C
C♯o
Em
B
E
G7
G7+
C
G7
C
F♯o
G7
G7+
C
B♭7-5
A7
D7
Dm7
G7
D. C.
al Fine

18
Etude

Composed by Frederic Chopin

Fantaisie Impromptu

Composed by Frederic Chopin

20
Military Polonaise
Composed by Frederic Chopin

Polonaise Opus 53

Composed by Frederic Chopin

22
Trumpet Voluntary
Composed by Jeremiah Clarke

Clair De Lune

Composed by Claude Debussy

24

Reverie

Composed by Claude Debussy

F+
Gm7
F+
Gm7
G9
C
D. C. al
Coda
CODA
E♭maj7
F7
E♭maj7
Am7-5
D
Gm
A7
Gm
A
Gm
A7
Gm
A7
Dm
Gm
A
Gm
A7
Em7-5
A7
Gm
C7
F

25
Pas Des Fleurs
Composed by Leo Delibes

C
Dm
G7
1. C
2. C
N.C.
p
G
D7
1. G
2. G
8

Pizzicati From 'Sylvia'

Composed by Leo Delibes

C
G7
C
B7
p
Em
D7
G7
C
G7
mp
C
D
E7
Am
C
G7
C

27
Valse Lente
(from 'Coppélia')
Composed by Leo Delibes

Serenade From Millions D'Arlequin

Composed by Riccardo Drigo

La Calinda

Composed by Frederick Delius

1. F#7
2. F#m7-5
Em
C7
Em
C7
Em
mf
E♭+
G7
f
C
Gsus4
C
mp
C6
F6
G7
C7
F
D9
Dm
Em7
Cm
Dm7
G7
C
G/C
p
C7
D7/C
mp
G7/C
C7
F
Fm
C
pp

O Sole Mio

Composed by E. Di Capua

Gm
F
C7
F
3
N.C.
mf
F
C7
F
p
B♭m
F
C7
1.
F
N.C.
mf
2.
F

Largo
('From The New World')
Composed by Antonin Dvořák

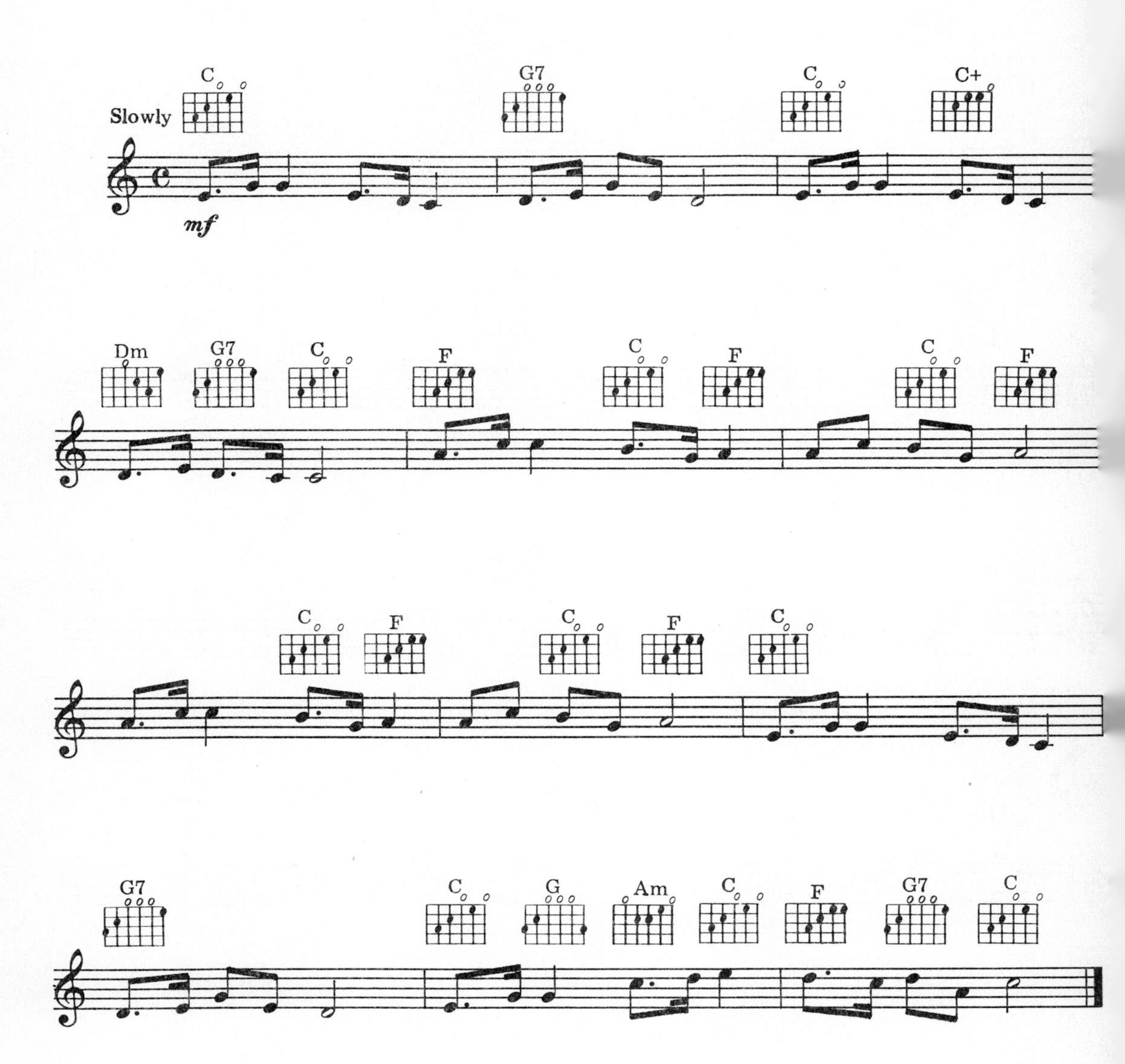

Songs My Mother Taught Me

Composed by Antonin Dvořák

Humoresque

Composed by Antonin Dvořák

F
C
Am7
D7
G7
C
C7
F
F♯o
C
G7
C
Fine
Cm
Fm7
B♭7
E♭
Cm
Fm7
B♭7
E♭
Cm
Fm7
B♭7
E♭
Cm
Fm7
Dm7-5
G7
Cm
Fm7
B♭7
E♭
Cm
Fm7
B♭7
E♭
Cm
Fm7
B♭7
E♭
Cm
Fm
Dm7-5
G7
D. C.
al Fine

Land Of Hope And Glory
(Pomp & Circumstance March No.1)
Composed by Sir Edward Elgar

C
G
A7
D7
G
A7
D
Allargando
C
D7
G
G7
f
C
D7
G
Em
rit.
1. Am7
D7
G
2. Am7
D7
D13
D7
G
ff

35

Chanson De Matin

Composed by Sir Edward Elgar

B♭/F
C7/E
Dm
F/C
B♭
f
F/A
A♭+
Cm/G
D7/F♯
Gm
B♭/F
p
C7/E
F
Gm
C7
poco rit.
a tempo
mf
F
Dm
Am
B♭
p
Gm
C7
F
B♭
Gm6
A
Em7-5
A7
Dm
Gm7
F
pp
poco rit.
accel.
B♭
B°
C7
F
a tempo

36
Poème

Composed by Zdenek Fibich

G7
E7
Am
Fm
C
Dm7
G7
C
E7
Am
Dm7
G7
E7
Am
Fm
C
Dm7
G7
C

Entry Of The Gladiators

Composed by J. Fucik

1.
E7
Am
E7
C7
2.
G7
A♭
G7
C7
F
mf
B♭
Gm7
C7
F
D°
F
C7
F
B♭
F7

B♭
F7
B♭
E♭
D♭o
B♭
G♭
B♭
E♭
E♭m
B♭
C9
C7
F7
B♭
E♭
D♭o
B♭
f
G♭
B♭
Eo
B♭
C7
F7
B♭

The Surprise Symphony

Composed by Joseph Haydn

Waltz From 'Faust'

Composed by Charles Gounod

A7
D
1.
2.
Fine
A9
A7
mf
D
A7
D
A9
A7
D
A7
D
E7
A7
D. C.
al Fine

Anitra's Dance

Composed by Edvard Grieg

Am
E7
Am
F
A°
Dm7
B7
B♭
E7
B♭
E7
Am
E7
Am
E7
Am
E7
Am

Largo

Composed by George Frideric Handel

C D7 G C G Am7 D7
G C G Am G A° Em B7 C
Am D7 G D F♯m7-5
G A° G Bm C D
A7 D7 G Am D C
Am G D7 G A° G Bm C D
A7 D7 G Am D7 G

Gypsy Love Song

Composed by Victor Herbert

43

Waves Of The Danube

Composed by Ivanovici

I Vow To Thee My Country
(theme from 'Jupiter')
Composed by Gustav Holst

Am G F G7 C F
f
C G Am G C G C
F Dm Am G F C Dm7 C F Dm C6
G F G7 C Em F G
ff
Am G F G7 C F G7 C

45
Spartacus
(theme from)

Composed by Aram Khachaturian

46

Mattinata

Composed by Ruggiero Leoncavallo

47
Liebestraum
Composed by Franz Liszt

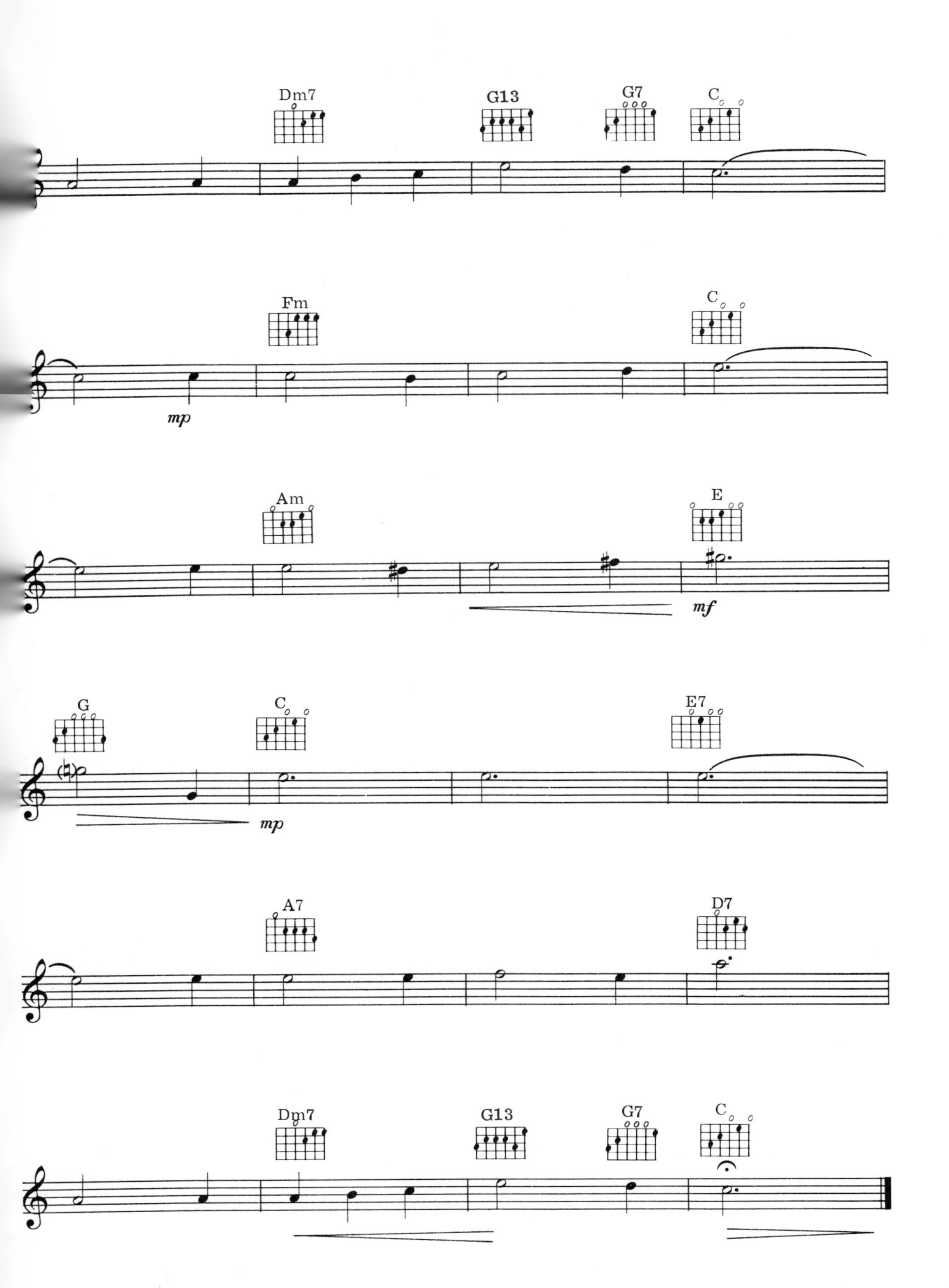

Dm7
G13
G7
C
Fm
C
mp
Am
E
mf
G
C
E7
mp
A7
D7
Dm7
G13
G7
C

48

To A Wild Rose

Composed by Edward MacDowell

C
C7
B♭
f
F
B♭
F
G7
p
C7
F
C
B♭
B♭m
F
C
B♭
B♭m
F
C7-9
F
G9
C7
F

Plaisir D'Amour

Composed by Giovanni Paolo Martini

Czardas

Composed by Monti

On Wings Of Song

Composed by Felix Mendelssohn

D7
B°
C
D7
G
D7
G
C
D7
mf
B7
Em
Am7
D7
G
G7
f
E°
Am7-5
D7
G
Am
D7
mp
G
G
D7
p
G
pp

52
Spring Song
Composed by Felix Mendelssohn

D
Dm
E7
A7
D
A7
D
A7
D
D°
A7
D
A7
Em7
A7
D
Am
G
Am
Dm
C
Am7
D7
D. C. al Coda
CODA
G

Symphony No. 40 in G Minor

Composed by Wolfgang Amadeus Mozart

D Gm6 D Gm6 D Gm6
sf sf sf
D Gm6 D Gm6 D Gm
mp
Cm
F7
B♭ Gm F7 B♭ F7
B♭ F7 B♭ F7 B♭ F7 B♭ F7
B♭

Sonata No. 15

Composed by Wolfgang Amadeus Mozart

Eine Kleine Nachtmusik

Composed by Wolfgang Amadeus Mozart

Turkish March

Composed by Wolfgang Amadeus Mozart

F7
Am
E7
Am
Dm
Am
E7
1. Am
2. Am
N.C.
f
A
D
B7
E7
A
D
E7
1. A
2. A

57

The Can Can

Composed by Jacques Offenbach

2. F C7 F G7 C F
mp
C 1. G7 C D7 G7
2. G Cm C♯o G7 G
Cm C♯o G7
C G7 C G7
ff
1. C G7 2. C F
G7 C F G7 C G7
C G7 C G7 C G7 C

Barcarolle Waltz
(from 'The Tales Of Hoffmann')
Composed by Jacques Offenbach

C7
Gm7
C7
F
F7
B♭
G7
C
C°
C7
C°
C7
D. C.
al Coda

CODA
F♯o
D7
Gm
F
C7
F♯o
Gm
F
C7
F
C7
F
C7
F
B♭
F
B♭
F

59
Caprice

Composed by Niccolò Paganini

Ciribiribin

Composed by A. Pestalozza

Dance Of The Hours
(from 'La Gioconda')
Composed by Amilcare Ponchielli

O, My Beloved Father
(from 'Gianni Schicchi')
Composed by Giacomo Puccini

Musetta's Waltz
(from 'La Bohème')
Composed by Giacomo Puccini

Scheherazade
(theme from)
Composed by N. A. Rimsky-Korsakov

Am6
D7
C
B7
A°
Em7
D
Fm6
C
Cm6
G
Cm6
G
D°
Am7
D7-9
G

65
Song Of India
Composed by N.A. Rimsky-Korsakov

C
F9
C
G7
C
A♭7
C
G7
F°
Am
E7+
f

C
C7
F
mf
B♭7
C
G13
C
Am
C
F
Fm
C
Cm
C
3
C7
F
A♭7
C
G7
C
ff

My Heart At Thy Sweet Voice

Composed by Camille Saint-Saëns

William Tell Overture

Composed by Gioacchino Rossini

F
C7
D. S. al Coda
f
CODA
F
F
A7
B♭
f
F
C7
F
C7
1.
2.
F
C7
F

Melody In F

Composed by Anton Rubinstein

F#o
G7
Dm7
G7
C
Fm
C
Fm
C
Fm
C
Fm
C7
F
C7
F
F#o
mp
Gm7
C7
F
C7
F
C7
F
D7
Gm7
C7
F

Gymnopédie No.1

Composed by Erik Satie

Em
D
Dm7
D
al Coda
Em
F♯m
Bm
Am
D
D. C. al Coda
CODA
Em
Bm7 /E
Am7
Dm

Moment Musical

Composed by Franz Schubert

Gm
D7
Gm
D7
Gm
E♭
G7
Cm
Gm
D7
Gm
Cm6
C#o
Gm
D7
Gm
Cm6
C#o
G
D7
G
D7
G
D7
G
D7
G
D7
G

The Unfinished Symphony
(theme from)

Composed by Franz Schubert

72

For He Is An Englishman!

Composed by Arthur Sullivan

Träumerei

Composed by Robert Schumann

D7-9
D7
Gm
B♭
A7-9
A7
Dm
Dm7
G7
C13
C7
D. S. al Coda
CODA
D7
G7
F
Gm7
C7
F

The Happy Farmer

Composed by Robert Schumann

D7
G
G
D
G
D7
G
Am7
D7
Am7
D7
G
C
G
D7
G
D7
G

Radetzky March

Composed by Johann Strauss

D
G7
C
f
F
G7
C
Fine
F
mf
sempre stacc.
C
G
G7
F
C
G
G7
G9
C
G
G7
F
C
E7
Am
E7
Am
E
Am
E
Am
E
Am
E
Am
E
D.S. al Fine
f
mf

Blue Danube

Composed by Johann Strauss

D7
G
D7
Em
Am
D7
G
D.C. al Coda
CODA
G7
C
G
D7
G
1.
D7
G
G7
2.
D7

G
E7
Am
G
D7
G
D7
G
E7
Am
G
D7
G
Am
D7
G

77
Waltz
(from 'Die Fledermaus')
Composed by Johann Strauss

78
Artist's Life
Composed by Johann Strauss

G9
G7
C
Fine
G
G+
Am
D7
G°
G
B7
E7
Am
F♯m7-5
Em
B7
Em
Am
G
1
D7
G
2
D7
G
D.C. al Fine

Tales From The Vienna Woods

Composed by Johann Strauss

D°
F
C7
F
C7
F
C7
F
F7
B♭
C7
F
B♭
Cm7
B♭
F7
B♭
Cm7
B♭
F7
B♭

Roses From The South

Composed by Johann Strauss

Kaiser Waltz

Composed by Johann Strauss

Capriccio Italienne

Composed by Peter Ilyich Tchaikovsky

83
Romeo and Juliet
Composed by Peter Ilyich Tchaikovsky

Dance Of The Swans
(from 'Swan Lake')
Composed by Peter Ilyich Tchaikovsky

85

Waltz
(from 'Serenade For Strings')
Composed by Peter Ilyich Tchaikovsky

Piano Concerto No. 1

Composed by Peter Ilyich Tchaikovsky

'Swan Lake'
(theme from)

Composed by Peter Ilyich Tchaikovsky

Pathétique
(from the 6th Symphony)

Composed by Peter Ilyich Tchaikovsky

Waltz Of The Flowers

(from 'The Nutcracker')

Composed by Peter Ilyich Tchaikovsky

Dance Of The Sugar Plum Fairy

(from 'The Nutcracker')

Composed by Peter Ilyich Tchaikovsky

F♯7
B7
E7
A7
D7
G
B7
Em
B7
Em
B7
Em
B7
Em
B7
Em
F♯m7-5
B7
Em7
B7
Em
Em7
A
Am
Em
Am
Em
F♯7
B7
E7
A7
D7
G
B7
Em

Serenade

Composed by Enrico Toselli

La Donna E Mobile

(from 'Rigoletto')

Composed by Giuseppe Verdi

Caro Nome
(from 'Rigoletto')
Composed by Giuseppe Verdi

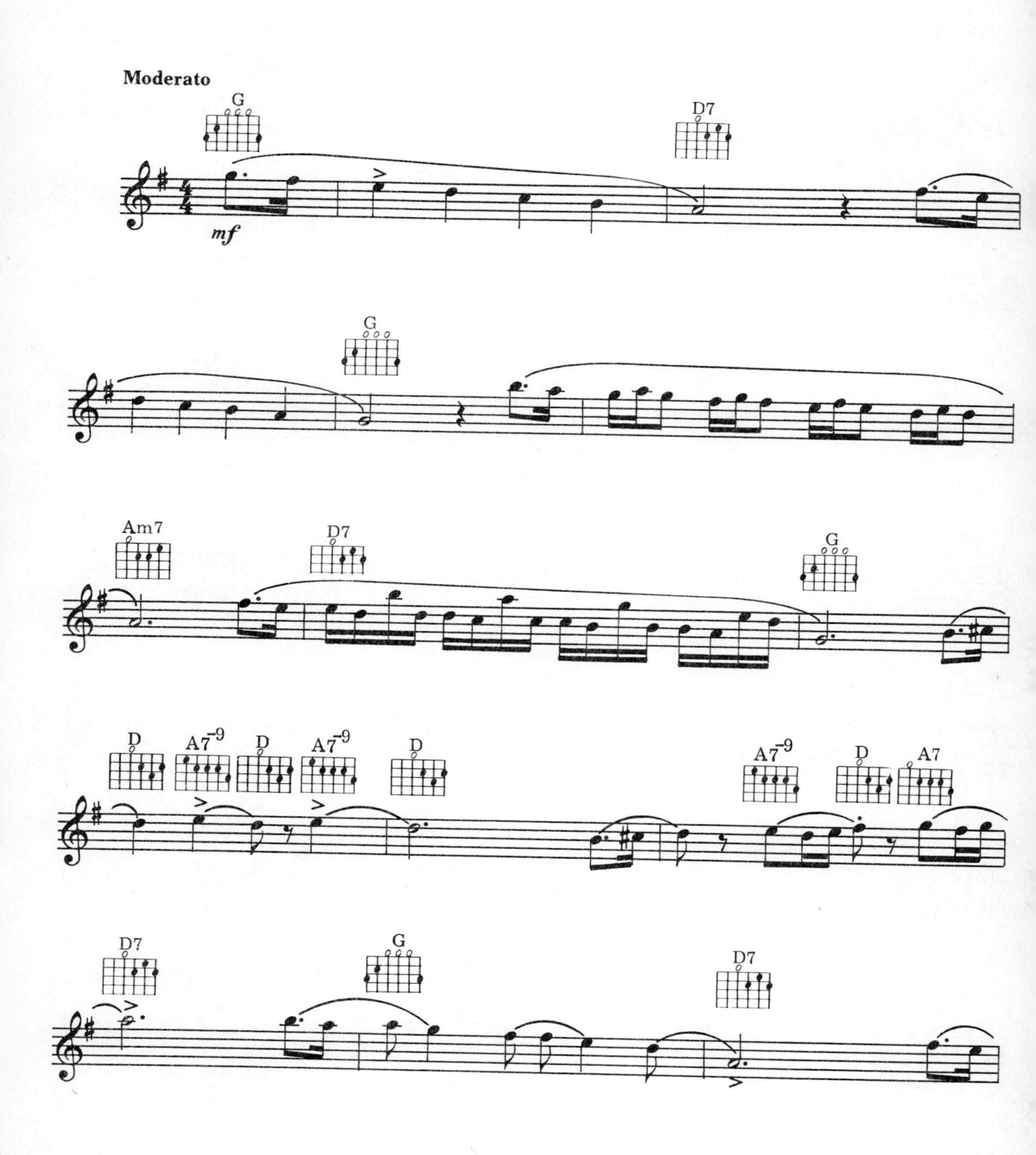

G
D
A7
D
A7
D
A7
D
A7
D
G
D7
G
E♭
B♭
Cm
G
A♭
E♭
G
E♭
B♭
Cm
G
A♭
D7
G

Anvil Chorus
(from 'Il Trovatore')
Composed by Giuseppe Verdi

Pilgrims March
(from 'Tannhäuser')

Composed by Richard Wagner

Bridal Chorus

Composed by Richard Wagner

Santa Lucia

Traditional

Dolores Waltz

Composed by Emil Waldteufel

Gm
Dm
A
E7
A
A7
Dm
A7
Dm
Gm
D7
Gm
A7
Dm
Gm
Dm
A7
Dm

99

The Skater's Waltz

Composed by Emil Waldteufel

Em
G7
C
G7
C
C7
F
Fm
C
G7
1. C
2. C
D7
G7
C
Tempo come primo
mf
G7
Cmaj7
Am
Dm
G7
C

Invitation To The Dance

Composed by Carl Maria Von Weber

al Coda
F
F
p
C7
F
C7
F
B♭
A+
B♭
G7
C
F
m7
G13
G7
C
2nd time D.S. al Coda
C7
F
C7
F

101

Greensleeves

Traditional